OCT 19

THE STORY OF HANUKKAH

BY BARBARA M. LINDE

Gareth Stevens
PUBLISHING

Please visit our website, www.garethstevens.com. For a free color catalog of all our high-quality books, call toll free 1-800-542-2595 or fax 1-877-542-2596.

Library of Congress Cataloging-in-Publication Data

Names: Linde, Barbara M., author.
Title: The story of Hanukkah / Barbara M. Linde.
Description: New York : Gareth Stevens Publishing, [2020]
| Series: History of our holidays | Includes index.
Identifiers: LCCN 2018052425| ISBN 9781538238745 (pbk.)
| ISBN 9781538238769 (library bound) | ISBN 9781538238752 (6 pack)
Subjects: LCSH: Hanukkah–Juvenile literature.
Classification: LCC BM695.H3 L55 2020 | DDC 296.4/35–dc23
LC record available at https://lccn.loc.gov/2018052425

Published in 2020 by
Gareth Stevens Publishing
111 East 14th Street, Suite 349
New York, NY 10003

Copyright © 2020 Gareth Stevens Publishing

Designer: Laura Bowen
Editor: Barbara Linde

Photo credits: Cover, pp. 1 Maglara/Shutterstock.com; pp. 2–24 (background texture) secondcorner/Shutterstock.com; pp. 3–24 (background flags) saicle/Shutterstock.com; p. 5 (top) Liana Elise/Shutterstock.com; p. 5 (bottom) Dmitriy Feldman svarshik/ Shutterstock.com; p. 7 De Agostini/Biblioteca Ambrosiana/De Agostini Picture Library/ Getty Images; p. 9 (main) Wikitiki89/Wikimedia Commons; p. 11 Sean Locke Photography/ Shutterstock.com; p. 13 (top) GreenArt/Shutterstock.com; p. 13 (bottom) Africa Studio/ Shutterstock.com; p. 15 (dreidel) Katrina Wittkamp/Photodisc/GettyImages; p. 15 (coins) Evan-Amos/Wikimedia Commons; p. 17 Hiya Images/Corbis/VCG/Corbis/Getty Images; p. 19 Monkey Business Images/Shutterstock.com; p. 21 (top left) iPixela/Shutterstock.com; p. 21 (top right) Noam Armonn/Shutterstock.com; p. 21 (bottom) Digital First Media/ Orange County Register/Digital First Media RM/Getty Images.

Printed in the United States of America

CPSIA compliance information: Batch #CS19GS: For further information contact Gareth Stevens, New York, New York at 1-800-542-2595

CONTENTS

Boldface words appear in the glossary.

Long, Long Ago

The story of Hanukkah, or Chanukah, begins thousands of years ago. The Jewish people lived in their homeland of Israel, or Judea, but they didn't rule their country. The king of Syria ruled there. He didn't let the Jewish people practice their **faith**.

present-day Judea

5

The People Fight Back

The king's army went to the city of Jerusalem in Judea. They killed many Jews. They did not treat the Jewish **temple** with respect. A Jewish priest and his five sons formed an army. They were called the Maccabees. They chased the Syrians away.

7

The Miracle of the Oil

The Jews took their temple back. They wanted to light the lamp, or menorah, but there was only enough oil for one night. Still, the lamp burned brightly for eight nights. It was a **miracle**! This is why Hanukkah is called The **Festival** of Lights.

the First Temple in Jerusalem

9

Eight Special Days

Hanukkah takes place in late November or in December. The exact dates are different every year, but it's always for eight days. Families spend time together. They follow some special **traditions**. One of these is telling the story of the Maccabees.

Traditional Foods

Families and friends eat meals together during Hanukkah. Potato pancakes called *latkes* are a traditional food. So are *sufganiyot*, or jelly doughnuts. Both foods are fried in oil. The oil is a **symbol** of the oil that burned in the temple menorah for eight nights.

latke

sufganiyot

The Dreidel Game

The dreidel game uses real pennies or chocolate coins called gelt. Players take turns spinning the dreidel. They read the **Hebrew** letter and do what it says. Players get all, none, or half of the coins. Or they add another coin.

Giving and Getting Gifts

Families have different gift traditions. The children may get a little bit of gelt each night. Some families give away their used clothes, toys, or other useful goods. There may be one big family gift, or there may not be any gifts.

Lighting the Menorah

Today's menorahs hold nine candles. The highest candle, often in the middle, is used to light the other candles. On the first night, a candle is put in the far right holder and lit. One more candle is added and lit from right to left every night.

Happy Hanukkah!

Every night, people say a **blessing** over the candles of the menorah. Next, they say a blessing for the miracle. Groups put on plays and sing songs about Hanukkah. Families bake cookies shaped like stars and menorahs. People say "Happy Hanukkah!" to each other.

GLOSSARY

blessing: asking a god to protect a person or a thing

faith: belief in a god or a religion

festival: a holiday event or celebration

Hebrew: a language of the Jewish people

miracle: an unusual event that people believe a god made happen

symbol: a picture, shape, or object that stands for something else

temple: a building for worshipping, or praying to, a god

tradition: a long-practiced custom

FOR MORE INFORMATION

BOOKS

Ganeri, Anita and Rachael Phillips. *The Hanukkah Story.* Chicago, IL: Tulip Books, 2018.

Trueit, Trudy Strain. *Hanukkah.* Mankato, MN: The Child's World. 2014.

WEBSITES

What Is Hanukkah?
www.chabad.org/holidays/chanukah/article_cdo/aid/102911/jewish/What-Is-Hanukkah.htm
Learn the history of the holiday, and look at photographs of people celebrating it.

JewishKids.org-Chanukkah Play 4:03
www.chabad.org/multimedia/media_cdo/aid/219022/jewish/Chanukah-Play.htm
Watch a play about the meaning of Hanukkah, put on by kindergarten students.

Publisher's note to educators and parents: Our editors have carefully reviewed these websites to ensure that they are suitable for students. Many websites change frequently, however, and we cannot guarantee that a site's future contents will continue to meet our high standards of quality and educational value. Be advised that students should be closely supervised whenever they access the internet.

INDEX